MW00579300

Libérate

Moments of Strength
& Perseverance

For the Reader:

Due to the content and the author's writing style, we have included a glossary for your convenience at the end of the book.

This book is composed of blog posts.

The moments captured by the author were experiences she endured and wanted to share. Each moment is based on her story and her sentiment at the time.

Libérate

Moments of Strength
& Perseverance

LINDA SOKOL FRANCIS
BROOKFIELD LIBRARY
3541 PARK AVENUE
BROOKFIELD, IL 60513
(708) 485-6917

Michelle N. Ramírez

Copyright © 2020 Michelle N. Ramírez

Published and distributed in the United States by Rose Gold Publishing, LLC.

All rights reserved. No part of this book may be reproduced or transmitted in any form or by any means, electronically or mechanically, including photocopying or recording without prior written consent by the author or the publisher of record.

The information contained in this book is based on the life experiences and opinions perceived and expressed by the author.

To protect the privacy of others, certain names and details may have been changed.

ISBN-13: 978-1-952070-07-5

Printed in the United States of America.

Book cover designed by Horacio Acevedo.
https://www.aceve.do/

www.rosegoldpublishingllc.com

Acknowledgements

From the bottom of my heart, I am grateful for my friends and family that have stood by me as I figured out my next steps in life.

I thank all of you who have supported my wildest dreams and have held genuine conversations with me.

I am grateful to those that offered monetary support, or that have provided me with unconditional love. I want to thank my parents that scorn me and do their best to guide me and my siblings, who are my main reason to live a life of poise, and my friends who became family and trust me with their house key if I need a place to feel safe and loved, and to those who graciously join me in my path to self-liberation.

To my dear friend Luis Narvaez, who's most considerable support made this book possible.

I thank you in the purest of ways and from the bottom of my ever-growing heart.

Dedication

Para las millones de mujeres que se ponen las pilas cada día, I dedicate this book to you...

To all the beautiful, strong women of color, who through struggling, succeeding, and building themselves, continue to hustle to attain their highest potential.

We often need a reminder that we are beautiful, unique, and that our presence matters.

This is for you - this is for me- for all of us.

Table of Contents

I loved you.

I loved me.

In loving you, I lost the love for me.

Libérate

Introduction
January 17, 2018

I told myself and have shared with others, my interest in blogging during this past year and a half. However, with procrastination and the ups and downs of life, I haven't made it happen.

Now, here I am reading Bianca Cotton's book "A Journey Through A Beautiful Mind," looking at inspiring quotes, listening to the meeting going on outside my office space, these are conversations regarding the development of a healthy community.

This is all so refreshing and the reason why I fight to liberate myself; the reason I am who I am and why I'm working on becoming the Chingona, Cabrona, and Chillona Latina Mujer I want to be.

I welcome you to join me in reading my experiences. I will go on tangents and rants, but that's okay. At the heart of this expression, is who I am. This is me in my path to self-liberation with the need to *breathe peacefully*.

I will primarily focus on my journey, on the role that mental health has had in my life and the presence of

Libérate

those I love the most, on what it means to be a 23-year-old Latina striving to end the toxicity and deadly act of machismo while not burning out and further exploring the concept of self-love.

Just as I have my own story that is compiled of many other stories, you also have a story inside of you. We all have a story that is worth sharing. It's worth it because regardless of how similar our stories are, they are unique to each of our beings. The magic here is that we are not alone. Even if it seems like we are at times, we honestly are not, and together, we can find this inner peace and self-love while also being that reaching hand for others in hopes that they move forward with us.

This is me. Let's go!

Libérate

Night Reflection
January 17, 2018

Sometimes I am just exhausted. I am physically and emotionally drained from explaining myself and trying to justify my actions and my thoughts. I want to inhale and to exhale purely, to let my body sink into the mattress, to float, to be a bubble drifting on and about.

I am tired of explaining to my parents why I want the partner that I do, or why I chose the major or career path that I did.

All I can do at times is take in our differences in opinion and breathe.

The thing is, I know that what I am doing is the best option for myself and my journey at this time. If I make a 'mistake,' I hope I will learn, or maybe I won't. Either way, these are experiences we must all go through.

I believe that everything in my life happens for a reason, whether good or bad. I am not religious, nor do I pretend to be. I am spiritual. I do my best to remain grounded, to burn sage, to be intentional and aware. Some may call this heading down the 'bruja' path, but it is more of a healing journey.

I have learned to appreciate and validate the perspectives of others and to understand that intention and impact may derive from the purest of love but that it also might very well not.

I don't have all the answers, nor do I have it all figured out, but I am learning and trying. I try to do my best. I try to love purely and sincerely, to be strong, to move forward, to be the best version of myself, and to remain true.

However, if after everything is said and done, I look at myself, at my partner, at my degree, at the progress (a self-defined term), and if I feel complete, I am freed. I do what I think is right for me, what my tummy knows and what my heart desires. I use my mind to think critically, and I always choose what I feel is best for me.

Whatever hiccups come our way; we will be okay.

Libérate

Words of Affirmation
January 31, 2018

'Be good to feel good.'

'Breathe, be centered. Ground yourself.'

'Be love.'

'Be bold.'

'Be patient with your own process.'

'You are pretty.'

'You are you.'

'There is only so much you can handle.'

'Live your wildest dreams.'

Libérate

Sprinkle of Life
February 13, 2018

I love to reflect.

I love sharing my thoughts with people I know, and with those I don't. I love being pure and getting excited about community engagement and bonding. The fact that people can spend time together is compelling, and it's powerful because you realize you are not alone.

My Uber driver this morning was beautiful. I got in the car, and one of the first things she said to me was that I was a beautiful young lady. This is a stranger who doesn't know me and she said I was beautiful. That made me feel amazing.

Our conversation was short and simple yet so organic, non-profit oriented, and entrepreneurship focused. It was a depiction of two powerful, independent women of color that kick-ass to accomplish our goals. It was great, and then, just like that, we arrived at my destination, and I will probably never see her again. Or, maybe I will. That's the wonder of life, that is life. You don't know what can happen or who you can run into. Whatever the case,

Libérate

I am a firm believer that there is a reason for every interaction.

Life, in general, is very complicated. At 23, I consider myself a 'boss lady,' but sometimes, this boss lady doesn't know what to do. After mental breakdowns, mood swings, and panic attacks, I fight my way back up. I come back up because I still want to live. I always want to feel alive.

There's that little spark in me that at times may be put down, but inevitably, it ignites again.

I get a rush when talking about something I love or talking to someone that I love. I feel a sense of home whenever I am in the presence of my special someone. I love that. That feeds me. Because I am continuously enriched by that feeling, I want to be that for others. People are beautiful, and even the most troubled are special.

One is not born evil, but because of untreated traumas, tragic experiences, and horrendous things of toxic spirits and beings, some grow up surrounded by negativity. It is for them that we must also remember why we are here. If life is positive and brighter for us, it is 'easier.'

Libérate

If we are blessed with nurturing vibes, that's a lovely blessing not everyone has. Therefore, we have an absolute responsibility to share that spark of life with someone to the best of our ability. We are to reciprocate the love we receive with those around us. Not everyone will appreciate or understand you, but that's okay. As long as you know why it is you do what you do, and you can find your inner peace and happiness, your life will be fulfilling.

You are the definition of a 'boss lady' or a 'boss person' to keep it gender-neutral. But most importantly, you are love. I am love.

Libérate

Podcast(s)
February 13, 2018

Along with reading about mental health, going to domestic violence counseling, and meditating, I also love listening to podcasts. These are great and convenient and can be done on the go!

However, just like you can choose your therapist (I ask for bio's), you can also choose your podcasts.

These below are for your reference and to be treated as a living document.

- Five mental health podcasts by therapists of color

  Link: https://www.redefineenough.com/blog/5-mental-health-podcasts-by- therapists-of-color

- Insight Timer

  Link: https://insighttimer.com

Libérate

- Hello Hunnay with Jeannie Mai

  Link: https://www.youtube.com/channel/UC -lCjm6VLCotg5ZOfJ7xF9w

There is also something special about mental health work coming from women of color in comparison to white women. Women of color, Latinas in particular, understand the Latinx culture. Regardless of which side of the motherland you are born in, you have this specific understanding. Even though we all have different experiences growing up, there is this part of us that unites us in who we are and how we develop ourselves.

Libérate

Rainy Day
February 20, 2018

Not all mornings are smooth or sunny. Some are rainy and dull. But the rain does wash away the negativity and heavy feelings. It replaces those feelings and fills you with re-freshness, purity, and a clear perspective.

Just for a second, you feel like a powerful boss lady. Each step you take is thunder.

Then, you question, why is this 'just for a second'? You are a boss lady; you are always powerful.

I just drove my car by myself. I got to work by myself. I am safe, and everyone around me is safe. I stopped on time, counted to three, and proceeded. I am doing my best to work hard and live life responsibly and to make my days matter.

I called my doctor to get my health on track by taking care of my body. I then enjoyed a bag of chips, which was arguably well-deserved. I am drinking water, staying hydrated, breathing, doing my best to remain centered and to appreciate life.

Libérate

I love him; I love me. I love everything about us. Of course, no one prepares you on what it's like to date or live with someone with a mental health condition; no one teaches you about bipolar disorder or PTSD. No one teaches you how to shift to healthy adulthood when you come from a dysfunctional childhood founded in trauma.

Instead, they teach us to run away, to hide, to shake it off and pretend like it's not there.

But when you are there, when he is there, when IT is there, IT will not go away, maybe not ever. This is why we learn to cope, why we learn to know love, to accept love, to be thankful for change.

This is why we are put here on this earth, on this side of life. This is the reason why we are given a life, a chance to create an impact, to be the impact, not just for others, but for ourselves: our family, our romantic partner, and our children. Our body is powerful. And we must listen to it as it communicates with us.

We must kick-ass, and we must rise together.

Libérate

Communicate
March 15, 2018

Communication is key.

Talk to yourself and talk to others. Talk to your parents, your siblings, and your partner. Talk to strangers. Talk with purity and with genuineness.

In the context of a romantic relationship, talk to your partner. Communicate with them, see what's working, what's not. Chat about how to improve your relationship, what you want, if you are happy or not. Discover and learn what you need from each other. Can you change anything, can you be more mindful, more present? Be intentional in these conversations. Talk from your heart. Sometimes things don't make sense, but that's okay. Loose thoughts are real thoughts.

Appreciate each other, your existence, your dedication, and each other's emotions. Love them intensely and purely.

Love yourself the same way.

Libérate

Communication nurtures your relationship. It helps you grow together. It is the key to dissecting actions versus intentions. Vital to understanding the who's and the what's and the why's.

Communication is often left behind, taken for granted.

If you are like me, sometimes you can express yourself on paper more. Writing helps with clarifying emotions and understanding them. It is the best way to figure out what you want to say and how to say it.

If you are like me, write them a letter. Write and express your love, give detailed examples and be descriptive. You can read it to them, or you can have them read it. You can cry as you read it or laugh as you read it. You can sing it; you can draw it. Just practice sharing your realities, voice, thoughts, and being.

Just be.

Be love, be present, be humble, be pure, and be you.

Libérate

Being Appreciative
March 21, 2018

There is always someone willing to help. We could be feeling overwhelmed like all the adult responsibilities are forcing us down and deeper into the ground. You may wonder how long it will be until you are underground. How much can you take?

You try and work multiple jobs; you are there for your loved ones, you nurture the young ones, you empower and praise the boss ladies that are meaningful in your life, but what about you, who takes care of you?

Going from having your apartment, your pets, your spouse, your home all in one, to watching it dismantle and spread around. You are no longer complete. You are dull and sad. You feel like a failure, or maybe, you are a failure. You are a mess, but still, you are a beautiful mess.

Be humble. Be pure. Be honest. You cannot always do everything on your own, and you need to learn to accept that and ask for help.

Libérate

When having financial troubles, you take upon a third job. You are more than ever, a boss lady. But in the meantime, what do you do? You ask for help. You are truthful. I get on the phone and express that I am aware of my payment status, that I am trying. That I'm only one person with one body. I need time to catch up, and I just took a third job. I am trying. In a very kind and warm voice, he asks, "when do you rest?" He's a stranger. Someone was doing their 'job,' but asked about my well-being. And so, I joke and say that once my payments are current, that is when I'll be able to rest again. Just like that, I feel slightly better. This random person has now done what he could to defer my payments. He gave me time to breathe. I can now relax a bit more. I can rest (while working my three lovely jobs, of course!). He, who just did me a huge favor, has now reminded me not to give up, to push forward, to continue trying. He who does not know me, who spoke to me for 3 minutes, has helped me. I have been helped. I was cared for by a stranger.

I am reminded to take it slow, to breathe, to be kind to myself, to love myself, to take care of myself.

Be appreciative. Be reflective. Take time to process those who help you, who genuinely want to be a part

Libérate

of something positive in your life. As I sit in my car, the car I just learned to drive, the car I love because it is mine, the car I am paying for and have insured, I think of the weight that has just been lifted off my shoulders. I am overwhelmed with the kindness I was shown. This is awesome. This is the life I want to live. This is the ground I want to walk on, and this is the air I want to breathe.

This is where I want to be.

Libérate

Unknown
April 27, 2018

I want to take a moment to honor and cherish all the wonderful women of color that struggle and love so hard. The work and experiences you all undergo are overwhelmingly inspiring.

These women include our moms, our tías, abuelitas, our community organizers, and students of the world. Being a woman and being a woman of color is a radical act in itself. The machismo that shapes us as we try to find or create ourselves in a world that seems to be out to get us. We wouldn't be able to do the things we do without knowing that it is possible because other mujeres have paved the way, because there is power in numbers, in remaining one, and in continuing to be pure.

Libérate

Isolation
April 27, 2018

Fearless. Unstoppable. On fire. That was me.

At some point, I realized that wasn't me anymore. Instead, I was now full of insecurities, of questions, of feelings that I was a bother. That it was my fault my circle of friends was so small. But was it really or was it the hurt of your words that were starting to become so engraved in me?

"You don't understand."

"You listen to what you want to hear."

"This is what you wanted."

"You pushed me."

"You're manipulative."

"Don't play dumb."

"You wouldn't be good at it."

"What goes in one ear comes out the other."

Libérate

"You don't listen."

Your continuous description of me as 'Ditzy' to belittle me while alone and in front of others.

These are only a few of your ongoing excuses for using such words, your reasons for justifying your wrongdoings. Often, I wondered, was this toxicity you or was it the bipolar disorder, the PTSD, the depression at fault?

You were not evil. You were pure and beautiful. You were one of a kind. You were my perfect.

However, that perfection did not last, and it came at the cost of me losing my spark. You being mean to me meant me losing the spark that fired me up, only leaving little bits of who I used to be. We may never know where we went wrong, but at least I know where I went right. I went right in realizing that I, too, had depression. I, too, had anxiety. I, too, was developing a bad mental state.

"A healthy mind is a healthy heart."

Libérate

Sunday Fun Day
April 29, 2018

Sundays used to be vibrant and fun.

Sundays were family days spent with our baby kitties, spent drowning ourselves in pure wild love.

They were spent taking care of responsibilities, cleaning our home, shopping for groceries, and listening to scandalous, and romantic Latinx music.

They used to be nurturing, and rich in energy. They were filled with visions of our marriage, our future kids, our home, our life together.

Even though people often say that 'perfect' does not exist, our Sundays were perfect.

Now, they are dark, gray, gloomy, silent, and still. Now, I am in an empty house with a knot in my throat and heavy tears rolling down my face.

As I remember the crazy, wild, fun, and beautiful love we had, I am reminded that chapter has finally come to an end.

Libérate

Abuse vs. Accountability
May 19, 2018

We learn that strength is measured by how much pain we can endure, how much we can hold without breaking. It is not defined by how vulnerable you can be, how often you cry, or how much you can process and understand. Strength is one of those words that we must deconstruct to then reconstruct through a healing perspective.

For too long, I have been trying to define, to justify, to figure out the difference between abusive behavior and the effects of your mental health. I know you loved me, purely and wildly, at one point. Now you 'showing' that love makes me feel insane, it makes me develop anxiety and a sense of paranoia, sometimes even leading me to think that I do not belong in this beautiful world any longer. When you are distancing, and I can no longer read you, when you guilt trip me, manipulate me, gaslight me, then hit me with the "See you around young lady stay positive..." That is a mind-twister.

I find myself calling my therapist on a Tuesday morning because I'm at work on the verge of an anxiety attack! I'm hiding in the bathroom, making this phone call because my body won't stop shaking. I am finding myself distancing my friends so as not to put them in danger. What the fuck is this?

Is this justifiable because of your bipolar disorder? Your PTSD? Your Depression? What is the boundary with understanding and accountability?

I walked into my last therapy session with the hope of getting an answer to my questions. I needed to know whether or not your behavior was abusive for the past year or so. Instead, I was told that to not be victimized; I have to qualify myself. I have to decide if I am a survivor of an abusive relationship or not. But day by day, these mind games, the fact that I am so much healthier, so much more alive, that I can laugh, and smile and have fun with my friends, the fact that I feel reborn and re-nourished when you are not near me, reinforces the fact that I am a better me. The love that we had was not always abusive, but it did eventually turn into abuse.

As I continue to process this concept and my reality, I am still in awe. I am in awe of how clear everything was laid out in front of me. And I am even more in awe of how good someone can be at making you think that you are the problem and that particular

Libérate

toxic behavior is somewhat normalized and perfectly acceptable. People say time heals, but I guess only time will tell.

Libérate

Re-nourishing Your Soul
May 11, 2018

Timelines. Development. Details.

Breathing, nourishing your body, your mind, your soul.

You are one. You are complete. Indulge in positive energy. Immerse yourself in healthy spaces with healthy people.

Let your mind wander and explore. Let yourself be a pure kind of wildfire, a wild love.

You are okay. You are not shattered. Although you were stepped on and belittled, abused or not, you were crushed. Nevertheless, you are lighting back up. You are sparking your mind and your heart.

You are overwhelmed with the possibility of how much you can do. You are alive again. You are reborn. He is out of my space and almost entirely out of my life.

Libérate

You are becoming whole again. You are realigning with your purpose, centering who you are and who you want your future self to be.

Libérate

Nurture Yourself
May 17, 2018

Spend time in green spaces. Let the sun warm your face, and the wind blow through your hair.

Don't isolate yourself. Be with friends, with people that make you happy. Remember those that were and are always loving you. Love them back.

You are a firestorm. You are water in its purest form. You are the grass, growing green from the ground up. You are the blossoming flower.

I thought I was the wrong one, the dirty one, the one who always messed up and was at fault.

I thought I was not good enough.

Now, not having you near me, not having any communication with you, and hoping you are in another state as you say, I finally have the space to heal. You are away. Please stay away.

I now know that I am love, that I am kick-ass and love. I am wild, electrifying, and marvelous. I have so much more to offer.

Libérate

I am good. I am me, and this me is enough. Perhaps not for you but it is enough for me. I got this. The fire in me is alive. I am here, reflecting. I almost bring myself to tears, just kidding. I do bring myself to tears because I have goals, because I am someone worthy of self-love, worthy of someone else's love, and I know it.

Libérate

Chillona
May 12, 2018

Sometimes I wonder why this is so heavy. Did you
consciously tangle me in debt for your appearance?
Did you really NOT try to do it all on purpose? Did
you think of me? What happened to your crazy, pure
love for me?

My body is heavy, and my eyes have huge bags, I
shake uncontrollably. These are my anxiety attacks,
my panic attacks? I hit myself, pull my hair. I
scratch my thighs and pinch myself. I want to feel
this pain. My eyes burn with hatred, for myself. I
don't recognize myself. ¿Qué me paso?

I cry myself to sleep. I'm tired. I want to sink into the
ground, into the soil, into the fresh and plushy grass.
I want to sleep in peace and not think of whether or
not my kitty cats are doing okay. I want to do my
errands without thinking that you might be watching
me, creeping on my doings. I want to breathe healthy
air and think healthy thoughts. I want to be healthy
and love myself and appreciate myself again. I want

Libérate

to be stunning for myself, to have the pure and wild love I had for you but have it for me instead.

Libérate

Self-care Monday
May 28, 2018

My skin is soft, a dazzling brown.

Tender like the frijoles my mami cooks.

The sun sinks into my skin and nurtures every part of my body.

My hair is thick and black.

A black, as rich as the strength of our ancestors will to survive in the taken land.

The wind blows right through singing freedom-libertad.

I shower in steamy hot water to open the pores. I exfoliate my skin washing away negative energies of those que hacen ojo, or those that simply wish to dull our sparkle.

Then, I run the cold water. I feel the coldness run through my skin. It's so cold; it makes me numb.
I brush my teeth, floss, and rinse.

Libérate

I wear a facemask for ten minutes.

I soak my feet in hot water because the tender roots are at our foundation.

My makeup is clean.

My face is moisturized.

My body is covered in baby lotion.

My abuelita's voice, so soft and tender. "Ay mija, cuidate bien;" que sea 'chingona' me dice.
Si abuelita, chingona como usted.

When we go to her terreno, abuelita carries a machete and slashes a branch off the banana tree. Como si nada. THAT, is a badass mujer.

Libérate

I Am 23
May 28, 2018

Can we talk about the lifestyle that is continuously instilled in us?

To have a family, we can call our own, and a husband to care for us while we also care for ourselves.

To have our child, a badass little girl that will kick someone's booty if needed. A small brown girl, happy and kind. Jumping in the water, eating cookies, and offering to share, to play with other kids. To play with mommy and daddy.

I am 23. I am still young, but it's not too early to start thinking of my perfect little family. It did not happen with him, but I am excited for it to happen with someone more fitting and deserving of me.

Now I ponder, is this a cultural pressure, or is it a vision I genuinely long for? Perhaps it is both.

I know I want to be married, to come home to my pets, and to my loved one. I want to be the one someone will do the impossible for. I want to be the one who will have someone come home to her, someone who will be loved and taken care of and can have the genuine love that I have always given.

I want someone who comes home to me every night and can share mutual friends with me. I want to be my own person with someone and not walk on eggshells near them. Something I am continuously working on is my fear of being alone. I fear not having anyone to talk to or to be around.

After making your life revolve around someone and not have the turnout that was so profoundly wished for, it's difficult even to see it as a possibility. Are they all manipulative liars? I don't know, but it is a risk worth taking. It is an empowering risk to face your fears, to take yourself out on a date, to treat yourself the way you want to be treated by others, to face alone time, and to combat feeling uncomfortable with it all.

Part of my anxiety leads me to take everything personally. Why aren't they responding to me? Am I annoying them? What do they think of me? Are the things I've been told real? Do they see me as 'ditzy'?

However, I am also aware I have these thoughts because of constant repetition; they became so engraved in me. Even though I have these thoughts, recognizing them is very powerful. Sharing this is powerful. Being fearless and a badass mujer is powerful.

Until the rest of my romantic life falls into place, I also have personal and professional goals. I want to be a peaceful and vibrant woman. I want to be kind to myself and the world, to fulfill my definition of success, and to be happy. That is one thing he taught me, that it is important to strive for happiness.

I want to impact the lives of others, not just our youth, but our moms, our papás, and tías and tíos and abuelitas too. I want to go back to my roots and always be reminded of where I came from and how I made it to US soil. I want to honor the struggles, and sacrifices of my parents and thrive as a badass brown mujer in this country.

I will work hard, travel, and achieve what I set my mind to. I have something to live for. I have to give back to my family, my mami and papi, the kids who watch me grow, and most importantly, I have to provide myself with the love and care that I deserve.

Eventually, I will publish my book and become a community writer. I want to become a community role model that teachers and children can recognize as someone who looks like them, who speaks like them, and someone who celebrates life like them.

I crave having a vibrant and growing community guided by those who work from their hearts, not from their wallets or political exchanges.

Through this and more, I hope to inspire others to pursue their goals.

Do that master's program, and get that Ph.D.

I will persevere and continue moving forward, not only for me but for us as a community.

Libérate

A Well-Deserved Escape
June 7, 2018

A México me voy.

Up in the sky, floating in the air.

Una milla más cerca a los que me me llenan el corazón.

¿Lloraré al ver la reacción de sorpresa de mi abuelita al verme? Probablemente porque he descubierto que tengo Corazón y soy chillona.

At last, I can recognize myself again. I breathe in deep, fill my tummy with air, and exhale.

Freedom. Libertad. Far away from the toxic stresses of life. Instead, I am going to where my heart truly glows.

La tierra de mis raíces, I am almost there.

Libérate

Process of Healing
June 11, 2018

It's funny and complicated how sometimes self-care can consist of thoroughly washing your hands and scrubbing under your nails, taking the time to soap, scrub, and rinse. Full hand washes and moisturizing after is so mesmerizing, similar to the process of healing.

Acknowledge your steps of progress. You are not stuck. You are coming out of your depression. You are becoming aware again and feel your spark lighting up again.

It is even more powerful to choose the spaces you want to be in, to choose the people you want around you, and to let go of those that dim your light. This is the power in being purposeful, strategic, and just being yourself, and feeling yourself sparkle. This is love. This is self-love.

Cheers to celebrating life!

Libérate

Chiquita y Preciosa
June 25, 2018

I used to be at a point where I wouldn't think twice about punching a wall.

I wouldn't think twice about scratching my skin, my thighs, my arms.

I would pull my hair. Yank it out, watch it fall to the ground.

Then, I would cover it up with some makeup and red lipstick. I would flick my hair, and I would pretend to be a vibrant soul.

I wouldn't eat, but I would make sure you ate. At one point, you would feed me, bathe me, brush my hair, and do my nails. You would choose my favorite lipstick tone to match my brown skin. We were in sync.

La morenita, chiquita y preciosa.

Libérate

Changes
June 26, 2018

It's amazing when your life isn't consumed by toxic people or their dense energies. This is when your life starts to change. Your body, your mind, it all changes by taking a lighter and healthier route. This is 'healing' or so I've learned.

My therapist said I am a 'firecracker,' so full of eagerness. She said I would be big, that I would reach my goals. I used to not believe it, nevertheless, I am believing in myself again. I'm bright, and I work tirelessly. I have ugly feet from working 13 plus hours with three jobs to prove it. No descanso.

I don't hate those that have hurt me or taken me for granted. I do, however, despise losing myself and losing my bright flame, that spark that I try so hard to instill in others. I see kids at work so full of life and dreams. They are little superheroes thinking of marvelous journeys to embark on. I love it, and it is because of that same love for my community and my people that I need to be one of them and not give up. I need to think of my own future and reach my full potential. I am alive. I am here. The rest, with time, can and will fix itself.

Libérate

I'm not complete sunshine. Sometimes I can't go two hours without waking up crying, heart racing, sweating, genuinely scared, and panting. Could I have developed some sort of PTSD symptoms from a toxic relationship or is this a panic attack? Do panic attacks even happen while you sleep? I don't know.

I don't know, but somehow, I do know I will be okay.

Moving forward, I will be much more intentional with who is in my space and their energy. Right now, I know my body is here. My heart and mind are healing and continuing to grow. Right now, I am out of that dreadful environment. Right now, I am the healthiest I have been in a very long time.

Libérate

Home
July 3, 2018

Defining my 'home' continues to develop.

It is no longer solely "home is where the heart is," part of it continues to hold relevance, but my heart is now elsewhere.

'Home' is where the kids fill the space with their laughter and chaos. 'Home' is where regardless of the impossible mission to please Latinx parents, they still choose to embrace you at your weakest. Home is where my mami me despide con 'I love you mija' o me dice buenos días con un 'mi amor' al final, where you don't have to have dinner alone or cry yourself to sleep every single night because you know you are no longer loved.

Home is where my mom shouts at you that dinner is ready and where my dad lays in his room or teases you about boyfriends, where my older sister coaches you about the wonders of life and wedding planning.

Home is where the words that once filled me with love no longer come from a lover, but my parents and my kids. My kids, the ones who lay next to me and share their warmth, spoil me with their love and attention because they feel my weak energy.

Home is not what it has been for almost the past five years, but that is perfectly okay as it is an ever-changing feeling and state of mind. 'Home' had turned into a toxic space that, instead of building me up, would have inevitably driven me to a life of unhappiness and depression.

Now, home means belonging, having a healthy place to sleep in a house full of those who will actually love you unconditionally. Home is family.

Libérate

Showing Love
July 3, 2018

Part of being purposeful and intentional with who I allow in my space and share energies with is deciding who I show love to. Not necessarily romantic love or interest, but a love of appreciation for someone's presence. It is a love that shows them that the world is a little different today and every day because they exist and because they matter to me.

When friends say, "I love you," it's different. It's a pure love that derives from a genuine place. You know they are kind-hearted when you go through life situations together, and although you may occasionally drift apart, you always come back together. Friends listen to you and let you express yourself; they are part of the reason why you are healthier now because they listen attentively to your goals, aspirations, and are always present with you.

Showing love is vibrational. It's a radical practice that you are alive and here with us.

Libérate

Friday the 13th
July 13, 2018

"Diviértete y goza lo que puedas!"

-Señora de la cafetería.

Translation:

"Have fun and enjoy what you can!"

-Cafeteria lady

Moral of the story: Celebrate life!

Libérate

Catching Up
August 5, 2018

It's been almost a month that I haven't written. Have I had thoughts? Emotions? Reflection time? Of course, I have. I just haven't made the time to sit and pour my thoughts onto paper. Maybe this means my coping mechanisms are being further developed? Perhaps I am not just surviving but I am living. I am more fulfilled and connected.

Here are a few thoughts and feelings.

Thankful:

As every day goes by, the closer and closer we get to Thanksgiving, I get nervous. I get nervous at the thought of expressing to my family how thankful I am for their love and support. Even though I have wild and random outbursts of positivity and negativity, I appreciate them being there for me. They are understanding and caring. They try to give me space, check on me, feed me, and love me.

Talking about what we are going through is culturally unacceptable. There are generational differences that are not at the fault of our parents, but more of a result of a different up-bringing. One of my greatest hopes is to eventually show my parents how thankful I am for them.

Exploratory:

Life is crazy, and I finally feel like a 23-year-old should. I am going out with friends. I saw a drag queen show, and I took a shot and a half. I rode on a motorcycle. I can drive myself to work and to the store, I can get myself a lunch during my busy day. I can breathe. I feel like I have potential again. I love choosing my friends and being surrounded by 'like-minded' people. I love talking to men and women who have goals and to supervisors who see the purity in my soul.

Most importantly, I love being connected to that purity myself. I love dancing, even though I don't know how to and I love breathing in fresh air. I enjoy engaging in intellectual conversations about policy, our Latinx identities, and our futures.

I love being, simply being here in the present but also thinking about the future. I love further dissecting different abuses and mental games I was subjected to. I am 23 and potentially declaring bankruptcy, and that is the most overwhelming thought currently in mind. But I am also 23 and have survived an emotionally, mentally, and financially abusive relationship. I am 23 and will be doing a second trip to a different country in a week and a half. I am 23, and my life will soon fall into place. I am still valuable, and I am not broken (maybe not perfectly put together, but not broken either). At the moment, I just am.

I am here, dog-sitting, sitting on the steps. The wind is blowing through my hair, reminding me of the endless possibilities that life has to offer. The sun is warming and loving my body. I know that if others can embrace me, then I can embrace myself too.

Revenge:

I cracked up when I first heard you hurt your back, part of me even wanted you to break it or maybe break a leg, or maybe stab your hand. I don't know. I just wanted you to be unhappy. I wanted you to suffer for all the shit you put me through, but these emotions are draining. Revenge isn't healthy, and my therapist says I'm not ill-intentioned. I do know you will get back the energy that you are putting out into the world. You get what you are giving. I am passed the phase of wanting you to feel hurt like I felt. I am happy, and I am healthy now.

Libérate

I can go for a drink and not worry about seeing you. If I ever do see you, I will figure that out later. For now, I am exploring, I am loving, and I am healing.

I used to hit the walls and punch myself. I used to pull my hair and slap my face. I wouldn't eat. I wouldn't laugh. I would obsess over loving you and why you didn't love me back. I had thoughts of driving straight into the wall, a concrete cement wall. The details were planned. I was all alone with nobody to see what I was going through.

But now, I am able to ask for help from Mujeres Latinas en Acción, a domestic violence agency for Latina women. My therapist became one of my greatest support systems. I wasn't manic, like other agencies told me. The family of yours that became mine too, they love me. They said I was just young and in love. You were messed up but you didn't have to mess me up. But anyway, now, I have possibilities in my life, and I love, love, love putting myself in spaces where I can thrive. I have that spark in me again. Others see that spark and light it up even more. I am passionate. I am pretty fucking amazing. And I know that now.

Libérate

Spiritual Formation
August 6, 2018

Feel the night sky fall upon you,

Release your inner body tensions.

Breathe in, count to five, exhale.

Close your eyes; feel your presence.

Imagine all your endless possibilities. Picture your life. This is yours to keep and yours to create.

You are here. You have an effect and influence on the world and those around you.

Your smile, the way you walk, the way you are.

Libérate

Advocating for Yourself
August 9, 2018

At this point, no one can advocate for me. No one can tell me what I need to do next in order to get my life together and proceed with peaceful days.

People make suggestions and recommendations, but little do they know that initiating the process of bankruptcy at 23 years old is draining. My credit life will temporarily be ruined. I am working 13+ hours on certain days through a total of three jobs to make ends meet because all of my time and energy are going to paying speeding and parking tickets that were not obtained by me. I attend court, see lawyers, cry myself to sleep because I cannot do this regularly. When you give your life to someone, and they talk badly about you, saying you are the abusive one and the manipulative one, that's beyond crappy. He's crying to his friends that he's hurt, complaining that he's trying to make it better. Yet he's okay with me having three jobs, even though my mental health is getting worse. I suffer from anxiety attacks which have caused many side effects. He's a despicable person and he will get what is coming to him without any contribution from me.

Libérate

In the meantime, I take a breath. I close my eyes. I give thanks to my many support systems. I remain focused on my well-being and the steps needed to ensure that I will be okay. Sometimes, I don't know how exactly to make that happen, but I do know that I am responsible for making it happen.

My therapist said I'm empowering myself by doing my best to figure out this mess, and I'm trying to believe that. Today is a Monday, just one of those days. But it is a Monday, and it is a day. So, when I remain appreciative, I remain humble. I try to sprinkle things with cuteness and sparkles. I am grateful for the numerous bendiciónes de las abuelitas del mundo, and for the positive energies that surround me. For you, I suggest you take a healthy approach and perspective and continue to shine as best as you can.

Libérate

San Salvador
August 21, 2018

During my first visit to El Salvador, I met my tío, his wife and children, and my abuelo for the first time.

Years later, I feel connected to my abuelita on my mom's side once again. When she visited me back home, we sat and colored in princess coloring books. We would dress up and play with barbie dolls. She read the bible to me, and I so much dreaded it.

My memories became so vivid.

I heard about the colors of the house my momma grew up in, and the stories of machismo, of violence, and of the many levels of disrespect women were forced to endure.

She shared stories filled with struggle along with their hunger for survival, one of the many reasons why our parents migrated.

Deconstruct the power in their existence. We owe it to them to honor and hold our culture dear to our hearts, nuestras raíces y razón por existir. We owe it all to them.

Libérate

Home
August 21, 2018

Home is a state of peace, and of nurture.

La amaca apapacha mi cuerpo; me carga y mece.

El chuchito, pipo, me sonríe .

Mi mamá se da unas carcajadas. Le sonríe a su hermano, mi tío. Sus ojitos llenos de amor y cariño lo mira con una ternura inolvidable. It's magical.

El cafecito con leche me da un tipo de satisfacción. El café (y la comida) une a familias de nuestra cultura.

Puedo respirar, suspirar. No tengo que tomar medicamento para dormir.

Solo hay tiempo para apreciar la familia. La belleza natural.

Deja que tus pies descansen. Que tú alma respire. Esto es un escape bien merecido.

Libérate

The Days We Fall
Sept 12, 2018

It feels like it has been a while since I last wrote.

I have been working 13-hour days (8 hours in a full-time position, and the rest as a sales associate in part-time retail).

My feet hurt. They are nasty feet again; they are small, wrinkly, and usually stinky. I no longer have princess feet. Things like this bring me down. I don't look cute or fun. I am almost always tired. I cry myself to sleep, and I have mental breakdowns in the shower on a regular basis.

Melatonin has been my best friend. I don't eat regularly. Nightmares are reoccurring.

All while I continue to be judged for choosing to distance myself from negativity.

I broke down and begged and pleaded.

I don't know what to do next. Life is not what it was supposed to be, and definitely not what I wanted it to be.

Libérate

Our Roots, Our Ancestors
September 12, 2018

I called abuelita not too long ago.

I love feeling the warmth in her voice. She's my abuelita.

I love talking to my tío, my prima, her mom, and the baby who is to come. They are great and a depiction of our roots and where we come from. They are the old versions of me, of my mom, and my sisters.

My cousin's tender voice asking, "How are you cousin?"

I love waking up to my primo's WhatsApp "Good morning" GIFs.

My primas asking me que para cuando llego.

I love feeling connected to each other. It is that priceless warmth of kind words, and of their presence.

Libérate

WOC as Rising Professionals
September 12, 2018

Women of color as rising professionals.

The brownness of their skin, walking the halls like they know they own the right to be in that space.

Every step they take is firm. They move with a sense of direction and with glow.

I hope they know what great role models they are and the impact they have on the world.

Libérate

Too Tired to Title
September 13, 2018

You'll have nights that make you fall, nights where nothing makes sense and you wonder why you are in this position. You question your worth, your intellect, and your potential.

Then, all the wonderful mujeres poderosas that construct your background and your roots, they come and remind you that you are a beautiful and unique creation. They remind you that life is about learning and growing, even when everything seems to go wrong, even when the universe no longer seems like it is aligned. You will be put together by the love that grows within and around you.

At some point all the nonsense you are going through will become a piece of cake, not because you are numb to it, but because you have learned and grown. You are stronger and fiercer than ever before. Until then, "imagínate cosas chingonas" and live your wildest dreams. You must keep pushing forward and taking baby steps. Don't give up. Ojo, una limpieza might also serve well.

Or maybe, just a hot shower with coffee.

Libérate

Pills
September 28, 2018

Earlier this week I went to the doctor's office.

I explained the lack of sleep, energy, and increased anxiety all while having three jobs, being on the verge of declaring bankruptcy, and trying to figure out how to close this chapter of my life.

I am impressed, I am proud of knowing that this disconnection I have is not due to the actual 'break up' but more due to the aftermath of him throwing me under the bus.

At least I am out of the relationship and the amount of self-hurting has decreased.

I've never been fond of the idea of taking pills, aside from birth control of course. However, Dr. Love says I might have symptoms of PTSD due to the toxic stress that came into play during my past relationship. She congratulated me for being a bad ass and for somewhat managing this chaos, but she still is strongly encouraging me to see a psychiatrist to confirm whether or not I have PTSD. She has also put me on anti-depressants medication.

Libérate

I am now officially on medication for anxiety, depression, and insomnia. This could all have been prevented if he took responsibility for his actions and paid his tickets, paid for the cars, and didn't leave me to fix his own mess.

Nevertheless, I am okay. Now I am taking medication and I am sleeping. The side effects have not developed, and I am doing what I think is the best for myself.

I am loving me while deconstructing some ideas of 'love' that had come to be.

Libérate

Fortune Cookies
October 5, 2018

The little slip of paper inside the fortune cookies became my small dose of hope. I would look forward to having Chinese for dinner so I could get one, open it, and learn what the universe had in store for me.

It was a small breath, a glimpse of the future.

Then that imaginary dose died. It slipped away, far away.

Now, I get Chinese and can let the fortune cookie sit there. I glance at it and chuckle because for too long this little piece of paper guided my life.

However, the universe does work wonders. While I was working at my retail job, a lady who I had met though my community work happened to notice me. I was slightly ashamed because within the nonprofit world, our work is so important as we have a direct impact on the lives of others. In retail, you can still have an impact on others but most of the job consists of watching out for snatch and runs.

Libérate

This lady, she told me I was a 'Luchona.'

I love that word. I furthermore loved being referred to as such. A chingona, a badass, a luchona.

Sometimes, the universe throws these little reminders our way.

Today, yesterday, and tomorrow, we are luchonas!

Libérate

Shining
October 10, 2018

I have been really reflective lately.

We had an amazing girls' night, from giving genuine foot massages to talking about our lives over dinner, it was a very meaningful night. Everyone was walked out to their cars because it was dark out and we all checked in to make sure we each got home safe, these are signs of true friendship and love. I can't help but reflect on these friendships that have nurtured my soul and helped me grow in positivity. When the reason you started to write has altered from a place of terror and pain to one of humbleness and purity, that is powerful and beautiful.

I love my work. I love working in Cicero and walking down the street and recognizing people. I love being acknowledged as a Luchona, with a capital L, by mothers who see me working hard.

Being happy with yourself and looking at your body and seeing your little lonjitas, your own ojitos y cachetes, makes you realize that you are beautiful and the marks on your body tell the story of how you kick ass and work for the future you want for yourself.

Having around the people who love you and share meals with you like family, kids, parents, tías, tíos, primos, and family friends is so special. It makes you feel like you are about to burst from the flame that has begun to spark again. That is the power of being surrounded by love, that is empowerment, finally being the firecracker ready to be mesmerized by her own power and love.

This means being one step closer to figuring out your life. Sometimes, we are put in spaces we never thought we would be in. We are faced with challenges that could very well have been prevented, but the universe works in mysterious ways and everything happens for a reason.

Let us continue to let our hearts guide us in the work we do and the impact we make.

This is life and this life is the only one we have. Therefore, we must be wise, humble, pure, and well intentioned. We must love wildly and purely.

Libérate

Self-Care
October 10, 2018

Self-care is realizing you need help.

Self-care is realizing you need a therapist.

It is acknowledging that anti-depression medication may actually work for you and your body.

It is realizing that PTSD is real and sometimes seeing a behavioral therapist or psychiatrist may be worth a try.

Self-care is putting yourself first and loving all that you are.

Libérate

Reviving the Soul
October 16, 2018

I feel my life changing.

I feel empowered, strong, and beautiful.

I feel capable of taking risks and sharing my knowledge.

I am appreciated by family and friends and I feel it too.

I feel loved, connected, and seen.

I am rising and shining.

I feel the spark in me light up, sometimes more peaceful than others.

I am always growing and exploring.

Libérate

Forgiveness
October 16, 2018

Sometimes you can forgive in your heart. This may help you find peace. However, whether you forgive the person is very much up to you. You must feel what you feel and embrace the beauty of every lesson.

We must let go of bittersweet anger.

We must not give them the power to control our thoughts or emotions.

We were once beautiful, together and then falling apart. Unfortunately, things happen, and choices are made. However, remember the universe only acts in accordance to how things were supposed to play out. We were never meant to be. I needed to see that I loved myself more than I loved you.

I have learned the love for myself is the purest of all.

Hay tantas mujeres chingonas, 'luchonas.' Son mujeres que reflejan la sabiduría y fuerza de nuestras raíces.

Libérate

Exhale
December 19, 2018

Exhale.

Feel your body loosen.

Look at your tummy grow with every full inhale.

And lower with every exhale.

Your shoulders feel like regular shoulders should feel.

Your manitas y piecitos are there, full of life and movement to help you do what you have to do.

You've kicked ass while having to pick up someone else's slack.

You must stop beating yourself up about it. The nights spent crying in the bathroom must come to an end.

This was a life lesson.

Libérate

You are now being faced with positive challenges in your career. You hold a position where you can make direct positive impacts on the life of others.

You can sprinkle your hope, love, and use your nurturing senses.

You are love. You are beauty.

It's fucking bad ass to feel like yourself again.

Libérate

Growth
December 27, 2018

I used to wonder what my kids were doing. Did they even miss me? What are my parents up to? What about my siblings?

My older sister has shared with me her concerns that we are drifting apart. She couldn't connect with me or talk to me anymore.

Now, my kids tell me what mischievous things they are up to. "The 'not fully lies' just "NOT THE WHOLE TRUTH." They encourage me to go out and be with friends. They're teenagers and I get to be part of their wonders.

They share the kindness in their hearts when they hug me and silently assure me. They know I've been working hard. They feel my energy but continue to love me.

My big sister knows me and loves me. She picks me up from parties just a little 'tipsy' and always listens to my funny and funky stories. This is our sibling bond.

Libérate

My parents and I have generational differences that are very evident. Pero aún así they stand by me and save me.

I've always wanted to be like those women that have it all together. Self-sufficient. Bold. Assertive. I continue to strive to be that woman.

Being single, I have enjoyed my exploratory phase in its totality. And maybe I'm not done 'exploring.' Maybe I want to continue exploring my sexuality, my body, my likes and my dislikes. All while practicing safe and consensual experiences, of course.

Although I'm far from being where I want to be, it's nights like these that I am appreciative of my growth. It's nights like these where I can watch movies and feel complete, where I can be surrounded by family and feel warm and peaceful.

It's nights like these where my job leaves me feeling fulfilled. I don't know everything, and I am still learning. I am trying as I continue to grow and challenge myself.

Libérate

I'm about to turn 24. I'm at peace. I'm happy. I can hear myself laugh, snort even.

I cry tender tears of happiness. My writing just comes to me. And it is this, being real to myself and others, that helps me feel liberated and healed. It is my tattoo that reads 'libérate' that reminds me of why I got it in the first place.

I wish with all my heart that women of color, all knew how far I have come in my interpersonal growth because of their influence, and their guidance. It is through songs such as 'Girl on fire,' or a TV series featuring Gabrielle Union, Gina Rodriguez, and others like Sandra Cisneros, María Hinojosa, and so many more that I begin to find myself again. To las Sandra M. Garcia, las Titi Karen, Titi Mariela, mi Tía Ellen.

Tonight, before my shower, I see my 'sexy' panties. It's been a while since I have worn them. I have realized that I want to wear them. I can feel sexy for myself and I embrace that.

Tonight, it feels good to be myself.

Libérate

Holiday Thoughts
January 1, 2019

Almost a year ago was when I started writing. It was January 17, 2018, when I started documenting my experiences in my last relationship. By documenting, writing, reading, editing, and reflecting, I was able to gather the shattered pieces of me, and start to slowly piece them back together.

Holidays were becoming so hard because I was constantly walking on eggshells and triggers were everywhere. Now, holidays are different. They are peaceful, calm, and filled with fuzzy socks, cafecito, sarape blankets, my loud family, the kids, and Christmas lights. It's my home because 'home is where the heart is' and my heart is here. My heart is finally in a space that, even through generational differences, nurtures my soul.

I have sat through a countless number of therapy sessions, doctor's appointments, and hours of figuring out proper medication or if it was even needed (it was). Me han limpiado con burning sage, they have saged my car, my spaces. I have slept next to bowls of water with a white candle burning, hoping it would catch las pesadillas.

Libérate

I have an appointment with a psychiatrist coming up and general checkups with Dr. Love. I will continue my medication and birth control porqué sigo de pícara.

I will keep writing, crying, and embracing las bellezas que tengo por ofrecer. I will continue to rise, shine, take risks, and go on adventures. I will continue to learn, grow, and explore. And finally continue to have fun and celebrate.

I will celebrate that I am beautiful, that I am smart, and that I read books and write to heal. I will especially celebrate life y liberación.

I will cheers to life and to my amistades del corazón, mi familia, y por siempre seguir adelante, regardless of the challenges forced upon us.

Cheers to all of us and to discovering what our futures hold for us! Cheers to healthy thoughts, productive times, and exciting stories!

Cheers 2019!

Libérate

Feeling Feelings
January 13, 2019

I have been feeling feelings. A lot of my feelings mush together to create uncertainties which then lead to thoughts and even more feelings.

Feeling feelings is real. Sometimes you do not know if the steps you are taking will guide you to your peace, or if they are going to dig you deeper into a hole.

You do your research, dedicate time for yourself, and surround yourself with like-minded people. You have fun, you enjoy and do rebellious things and get to feel like a regular young adult in her 20's.

At this point, I am 24! My birthday passed and I had such a good time with friends and family. I met boys and kissed them. I got on stage with la banda and finally, I felt like a regular 20 something year old. I am 24 and I constantly remind myself that I am full of life and opportunities. I can explore, I can be picky, and I can create game plans to make my crazy dreams a reality. By this time, next year, I promised myself I would have my book release. That is thrilling. It is a thrill because I get to be that stunning woman of color that hustles and kicks ass to fend for herself. I get to be that woman, that growing up, I so much admired. I get to be las Tania's, Carolina's, LT's. I attest so much of my self-empowerment and deconstruction of toxic masculinity and women of color feminism, to the women that were key in my educational experience. To those women who showed me I too could be in a university, a private white-serving university, you mean so much to me. I loved DePaul University and what they offered me and together we made it an experience that I would never forget. I am constantly reminding myself that I am bad ass and that I can do the unimaginable thanks to the powerful women that came before me.

However, self-doubting feelings still come to mind. Am I doing enough? Am I on the right path? Am I having 'too much fun'? How do I know?

I guess, you don't know and perhaps, this is one of those times when it is okay to not know, when it is okay to have these uncertainties. It is okay to feel overwhelmed. We need to allow ourselves time to process our own thoughts and understand why we have them.

Libérate

Me siento en la silla, con mi cafesito. I pour my feelings onto paper, and just like that, it all makes sense. I started writing to liberate me from a cycle of craziness. I started writing to start understanding that I am enough, that I never needed to hurt myself or feel less of myself because of someone else. I don't feel hatred anymore. I love my experiences and the times I have been full of life; this is just what living and growing is supposed to be. It is all a series of mushed up experiences, thoughts, and feelings. The best part is that you get to make them on your own. You get to be the queen of the castle, the roots of the heart.

This is it. This is life.

Libérate

Deconstructing Old Mindsets
January 29, 2019

This is all very mentally draining.

It is commentary like "La ropa sucia, se lava en la casa," or the belief that only certain women can wear tight or revealing clothing, and red lipstick. It's this idea that only some women can take up space or be confident that gets to me.

Other women can do it, but que no sea mi hija. Why? Why can't we have a wild self-love, or feel sexy, or embrace our bodies and the amazing things it can do? Commentaries that are directed to other women, are also a reflection of perspectives towards us. There are so many women in our families that are so focused on bringing down other women. ¿Críticas y comentarios como 'que escandalosa', 'parece una vaca' can this form of expression stop?

How do we make it stop? Is it possible to change these mindsets? Que no se pasen. Si se puede crecer y aprender. Nos podemos reeducar con disciplina. We must first understand that these ideas are derived from everyone's childhood and how they were raised. However, it is possible to change these perspectives through accountability and thinking better thoughts. We can heal from this. You can do this through compassion, conversation, and love.

If there is one thing I have learned, it is to pick your battles. If someone you love won't change their beliefs, if you try and try and they still won't budge, that's okay. They are distantly listening, or maybe not, maybe that particular individual is not going to change because they have some self-reflecting to do.

In the meantime, while everyone is undergoing their own process, take in your own process. I have begun embracing 'gordita pero bonita'. I am bonita. I am calmada pero cabroncita. I can take space and challenge myself, I can do things I never thought I could do. Mis labios rojos como la sangre con brillo en mis ojos. Curiosa y estudiosa. Soy niña de casa, pero igual me gusta andar en la calle. Me gusta la fiesta. Divertirme. Unas cuantas margaritas. Soy trabajadora. No me rindo. Soy escandalosa como mi madre y a la vez reservada como mi padre. Con un gran corazon. ¡Podemos ser todo eso y más!

Chingonas. Luchadoras. Chillonas.

Libérate

We are composed of the many stories of our roots and ancestors. We bring years of trauma, pain, and suffering through our vessels. We bring the struggle.

But we also bring the kick ass strength of our ancestors. We bring dedication and love. We bring energy, magical auras, and resistance. We are all of that and more.

The moral of the story is that we sometimes hurt because we do not know how to process our own traumas. However, the one thing you should never do is dim someone else's light, don't be that negative energy.

We are all fighting our own battles and we are each in different parts of these battles. We must support, love, and hold each other accountable during these times in our lives.

It is only through compassion and support that we will reach a true level of unity as a group of people, that for too long has been driven to think less of one another.

We are all part of a beautiful image. We are beauty. We are love.

Libérate

Las Mamás de la Comunidad
January 30, 2019

Es un honor poder servir a mi comunidad. Es un honor el que otros alreadedor tuyo te apoyen.

Pero es aún más un honor, tener mamás que crean en nosotros.

Las madres de la comunidad son las señoras de las tiendas, las mamás jóvenes, las mamás de edad.

Son las mamás que se organizan y aunque no reciban reconocimiento, siempre están viendo como poder mejorar a los demás .

Son mamás de sacrificios. Mamás con rayos como el sol.

Libérate

Reflection
February 1, 2019

Reflect.

Take time to think and process.

Embrace your nurturing energies.

Feel the richness in your soul.

Your spark is shining.

Your fire is lit.

You are becoming who you were meant to be.

Take pauses throughout your day and look around
you. Kiss the air with the beauty of your skin.

Have fun. Enjoy, sing, and dance.

Live.

Libérate

While I Should Be Sleeping, I think
February 5, 2019

Preaching self-care.

Drink your tea, take a hot bath, brush your teeth.

You may sometimes forget to do it yourself.

I absolutely love helping people. I love helping people down to the very core of my being. However, I have also learned that it can be risky to help people if boundaries are not set. I have learned that although I want a partner, I will not be their parent or their therapist. Of course, I will assist them in finding resources, but their healing process cannot solely be based on me alone.

You pour yourself into love. You give it your all. And sometimes you lose yourself in it.

I could not remember if I had showered or brushed my teeth. I couldn't even eat. I would look at myself in the mirror and see someone else looking back at me. I wasn't myself anymore.

Libérate

Though as time passes, it eventually gets better. The journey to finding self-love was what saved me. I thank the universe for putting people in my path who have supported me and held me. I thank you for letting me vent countless times, for late nights, and for loving me through my worst days.

I write. I own these feelings. I fail but I succeed, so technically, I have not failed. I have experienced life. I write to process my thoughts, and my experiences. I write to get in touch with myself. I write because this is the only way I am able to reconnect with the person I used to be.

I write to save myself. So many *beautiful* women helped save me by writing their stories and by being their transparent selves. I become overwhelmed con sus voces tiernas y llenas de amor. I become overwhelmed because I too have recognized that of my own.

Libérate

The Thoughts in Your Head
February 5, 2019

As time passes, your mind heals.

But thoughts linger in your head and when you least expect them, they come back. They talk to you. They manifest through nightmares and panic attacks among other ways.

One year later, and this still happens. I wish you knew the damage you caused, and not because you stopped loving me or fell out of love with me. Honestly, I must admit, I knew one was going to stop loving the other, but I always thought it would be me.

Part of me knew we were not meant to be, but I had to try until the very end. I had to try until I chose the love for myself over my love for you.

I chose to take care of myself, instead of watching you sink. I do not need to watch you sink.

The Earth's energy will take care of you in its own way.

Libérate

Sometimes I wish you knew how dangerous you are because of the way you purposely abused me: mentally, emotionally, financially, and physically.

You must know to stay away from those whose beauty you cannot appreciate.

You were supposed to be someone who loved and cared for me but instead you hurt me. You would leave me at home with nothing to do while you went to 'foster your friendships' con tú amiga la de la santa iglesia. You would hear my wailing for you to come back to me, to save me, but you never would. Instead you would yell at me and threaten to drag me out of the car. I was scared of you, and I was scared for my life because you punched a hole in the wall and who knew if my body or face would be next. You would sleep on the living room futon or lock yourself in our guest room because I was so unbearable to be around. What happened to the love you once had for me?

Do I still care? Perhaps, but I care more that you used your power over me to mind fuck me the way you did.

You know what I also care about?

Libérate

I care about how much I have grown. I care that I can look at myself again in the mirror and see my ojitos color de cafecito calientito glow. I care that I am reconnecting with my family and sharing my spaces with friends and other people I love. I care that I am no longer drowning in my tears, instead I am so overwhelmed with the wonderful souls that surround me. I care that little by little, I am taking steps to become who I once was. I am kicking ass and taking care of what I have to do. I am not the mess you left, but I am the luchona, chingona, chillona, coqueta, pícara, and cabrona, you thought you knew, and with grace I say, _____ who?

Libérate

In Essence
February 5, 2019

Write.

Write to love yourself. Write to heal, and to process.

Just write.

Libérate

Documenting
February 10, 2019

I write to analyze, to process, and to understand.

First couple of steps for the Ch 7 have been complete. The first check has been made. My lawyer maybe gave me a low-price to file because he lamented my situation or maybe because he sees there is good in me. Maybe he genuinely wants to help, to ease this confusing process. It suddenly does not seem so scary when you can put a face of hope to the bankruptcy. Yes, this will happen, yes, it will ruin what remains of my credit. But it will be okay. It is seemingly a smooth process. We have a hearing date coming up and then that should be it.

So much weight will be lifted off my shoulders.

My appointment with a psychiatrist is quickly approaching. In just a couple of days, I will be reliving so many traumas. Am I purposely causing anxiety attacks by going to see her? Will the nightmares intensify? I hope not, but I know these are both still partially untreated. I might as well figure out how to work with them.

After that, there's a follow up with Dr. Love. She uses a rounded approach that will check on every part of myself. I like that. She helps me feel whole again.

I have also emailed a former agency to potentially start therapy sessions again. I also have all my W-2s and can make an appointment for my taxes. This is good. My timeline is flowing.

Sometimes it seems rather silly and repetitive, but this is my reality and the reality of so many others. This pattern of behavior that toxic masculinity holds causes so much trauma in many of us. So many people believe that it shows strength to hide the effects of trauma, but it does not. We must always hold each other accountable in taking care of our sisters and brothers, our mothers and fathers, and everyone around us. From los tíos to los vecinos. We must take care of our mental health and stop these unhealthy cycles.

Documenting these steps, these small and wide-ranging accomplishments, is crucial for me. From self-harming to now, this has been a transformative experience.

Libérate

Each day that goes by, the light seems a little bit brighter.

Libérate

Oh shit - This is me
August 25, 2019

There is just something about walking out of a community-based coffee shop with my laptop full of great ideas to help our community thrive. I'm also wearing my glasses that make me feel smarter, not just smart!

I have enjoyed spending time with the like-minded souls in my community. I am surrounded by so many beautifully grounded women that are ready to kick ass, join forces, and make anything possible.

I walk towards my car with the wind blowing through my hair.

I think of the future, and of potentially exploring Ph.D. programs. The fact that I can begin to think of Ph.D. programs is amazing.

Life got tough for a little bit, almost two years actually. Yet, like Sandra said, I am the 'package' I seek to be. I am this package for myself, and not for anyone else. I am reconnecting to my foundation, to the kind of life I want to pursue, and to building the home I want to come home to everyday.

Libérate

I am finally identifying with myself again. This is the most powerful, radical, and intense love I have felt for myself in such a long time.

Pieces are falling into place and it's going. It's all going.

Libérate

Untitled
July 15, 2019

People's energies never fail to amaze me. The powers and spirits we carry have the potential to influence so many lives.

I went to a meeting at the UIC campus. I took the pink line to the Polk stop. I had genuine and odd interactions, a couple of good mornings and some awkward stares from others.

I feel good. I feel that little by little, I embody the woman I've always longed to be.

I got off at my stop and grabbed my coffee, of course. I ordered on the wrong register but nonetheless, the workers were kind enough to ring me up.

When you make it a point to leave early and give yourself time, you are able to walk lightly, enjoy the wind, and enjoy the sun being soaked into your skin.

Construction guys are working hard. One said good morning. And I responded with, "Happy Monday!"

Libérate

That was all it took to "make his day" and although part of me wonders if he was being flirtatious or just nice, I'm choosing to believe it might be a little bit of both. And why not? You attract the energy that you put out into the universe.

I didn't know why I gave myself so much extra time to get to my meeting. But now, here I am sitting in this small quad with benches dedicated to certain people. I hope I get a bench one day or maybe a tree, a tree to represent growth and exploration. They're green and vivid. They grow upwards, sideways, and are full of life. You must nourish them and love them.

There's this small water fountain in the middle. It's surrounded by flowers, leaves, trees, and all sorts of plants.

Most importantly, I am present with myself. I am writing and reconnecting with my soul. This is it the woman I've always wanted to be.

Libérate

Life Updates
August 25, 2019

Recently, I have been present in my life and in the life of those around me. When I say 'present,' I mean PRESENT!

I feel it, and I see it. I've been surrounded by peaceful settings, and empowering people. These are people who believe in me and trust me, and people who nurture my soul and continue to enrich my life.

I have felt loved, hugged, and nourished. The opportunities presented to me seem to be endless. But most importantly, and I cannot stress this enough, most importantly, I am feeling like Me. Do y'all understand the power of that? The power of waking up and going outside and thinking:

'Dang, I am doing it.'

So, let me update you a little bit.

After almost two years, I have finally paid off over 5k in tickets and expenses predominately collected by him. I have finished paying them all! My chapter 7 bankruptcy has been discharged; I am free of paying car tickets. Although I had a panic attack at the dealership, I was able to advocate for myself and I traded in my car. Just like that, I walked out with a 'retired demo vehicle' or as I like to say, a car that is only under my name! And no one else's.

I often think, did he do this all on purpose? Maybe not, but then, I pull my thoughts back and focus on moving forward; lo que pasó, ya pasó. Y se acabó.

My car is now a product of this experience, of my time, my incredible work, my strength and perseverance. The car is insured, and I am officially able to drive in Chicago. I am no longer restricted to the Cicero area. The compassion and understanding from the dealership workers was incredible. They calmed me down and made sure I was safe and okay, and thanks to them I was able to walk out with such a weight lifted off my shoulders. This is the same feeling I hope to give my families that come to me seeking assistance at work. My work is not just my job, serving my community is my purpose. I want to grant that freedom, that suspiro, that warmth to others, as it was given to me.

My poor wackos, he held me down outside a party while I cried my guts out. My dear Sandra, who has

Libérate

been such an essential role model in my life, from the bottom of my heart I thank you. To her sisters Titi Mariela and Titi Karen, their mamá, my amigas, my Maribel and Jennifer and amigos, thank you all for everything.

Although I was full of confusion and misunderstandings, you have all remained by my side. Most of all, thank you to my family. You played the biggest role in my liberation. I am not God-driven, but these souls are and always have been my biggest blessing and have helped pave the way to my liberation.

I am looking into getting a master's degree in social work or starting a different certification program. This includes Ph.D. programs! O sea, ¿¡qué es eso!? Eso es imaginarse cosas grandiosas. Eso es lo que podemos hacer¡ eso y mucho mas!

I am also halfway done with my training to be an interpreter in the state of IL. Even my piecitos are smoother! And those have literally served as my foundation! En algún momento, they kicked ass with 13-hour shifts! Now, they are being used for jogging and walking.

Libérate

I am taking more vitamins and drinking more water. My body is breathing and thinking healthy thoughts.

I still have a couple of hundreds of court orders pending, but opportunities are coming to me. And from my mom's couch, I might have my Jane the Virgin moment ahead of me. O sea, these bad ass, pure, experienced gloriosas, poderosas, chingonas, increíbles, dulzuras de mujeres, were foundational in me taking control of my life again. Whether or not, they know, I hope I can one day just thank each one individually. This might come as a fan letter or a Facebook post because I do not know how to get in contact with Gina Rodríguez for example. Pero, la que tiene perseverancia, alcanza. Así que, ahí veremos.

Libérate

Sharing Your Story
September 3, 2019

Sometimes I wonder if I am exaggerating.

Was my experience really traumatic enough to share with the public? Maybe a year or so ago with the help of very dear mentors, I decided I wanted to share each of my reflections. I wanted to publish this as a book. ¿Qué locura no?

However, there is no such thing as 'that traumatic' because this is not to be compared to anyone else's experiences. We each have different experiences and they are all equally as powerful.

For me, writing was really it. It was what helped me and although I could not delete my errors, I was able to go back and make adjustments or "edits" to my life in order to pursue the pretty rose gold life I want to live. I want to be happy, to feel loved and be loved and embrace it. Through this method, I am able to give myself just that. It is an ongoing process, but it is a process that does not have to hurt.

Re-reading some of my initial pages and even mentally reflecting on the ways I would self-harm, I know I have come such a long way. Now, I cry tears of joy because I am proud of myself, because I have learned and grown. Of course, there will be other challenges that are yet to come, but at least I know that I am more than capable of facing them and I am even more certain of who I am. I continue to make mistakes at times, but the learning and growing component is key. I am not perfect, but I try my best to be one of those souls that feels types of energy and can guide people if needed, all while maintaining my boundaries. If it gets too toxic for me, I will respectfully decline.

I have always said that if I can help save just one person, my purpose for being put on this Earth will have been fulfilled. If I can just change or inspire one person, I will live through them. In the case of my absence, they will have a little piece of me. If that person is you then, I love you and it is now your duty to replicate that love and inspiration for someone else. That is the magic of our souls being connected, we are able to sprinkle our dust onto others and embed in them this genuine intentional aspect of love. Then they can care for someone else, who can care for someone else, and on and on and on. This is the domino effect of healing.

Libérate

I hope you remember, that your story is real. Your emotions and feelings are always valid. Just because our families have experienced different traumas and have survived toxic behavior, does not to any extent mean that you have to do so as well.

I hope you remember, that you are important. People, who you may not even know, love you. I hope you know that it's okay to be picky with your therapist and ask for bio's. It is okay to challenge your workspaces, and the family you allow near you. Most of all, it is definitely okay to challenge your life partner.

Please remember that self-love and self-care is the most powerful, radical love you can feel, and that you are so worthy of reaching your wildest aspirations.

Con eso, Libérate.

Libérate

Next Steps
September 18, 2019

An appointment has been confirmed with a woman of color therapist. I updated my doctor that I do not want medication for anxiety but rather I want to take care of myself through counseling services. However, I am opened to both if they are needed.

After rescheduling two initial appointments with my first psychiatrist referral, I asked for another one. The third try was the charm!

This one is at the UIC campus. After a back and forth, answering triggering questions, calls and email communication, we were able to confirm my medical insurance. Mental health services are not easy to attain. Now, I am more comfortable going to this visit and seeing what my psychiatrist suggests. This sounds uneasy to me but ahí le vamos.

Work is going and I am glowing. We are running, jogging, walking. We are learning and thriving. We are getting there. Pasito a pasito.

Libérate

Rose Gold Publishing, LLC
September 19, 2019

This is it. I am furthering a goal of mine to share my experience with my community. I am publishing my book, my story.

I am sharing a very intimate part of me. A part I hated with such a strong feeling. This part took me to such a dark place, from crying on the street to developing and coping with anxiety and panic attacks.

This part of me is still traumatized. This part of me along with my experience with machista and toxic men thus far, has made me more cautious and protective of myself.

However, this part of me was also key to reaching my liberation. This part of me connected me to my emotional self, and through this I learned to cry and fuck it all. Through this I developed an even more genuine connection with myself and those around me. I learned to love myself and my body. I learned that I can kick ass and glow.

This is a part of me that I am choosing to share, even though I'm scared, and I'm nervous.

Libérate

Denise Pedroza Sandoval, one of my kindhearted friends, when I shared my feelings on publishing, she said 'Pero, why did you start writing Michelle?' Y con éso, this is me.

Feel free to write to me, to share your thoughts with me. I love genuine love and people. If I can ever be of service, I will try my very best to do so. I tell my sister, when you have even a little bit, that is more than others, and so you must share. We must practice what we teach our children.

Genuineness and kindness are key.

Libérate

A Little Bit of Everything
November 02, 2019

Why is it easiest to write when you are upset or overwhelmed with heavy feelings?

I want to write when I am happy, or overjoyed. Sometimes I do, but perhaps when you are more excited, joyous, and happy, you are also more present. In which case, it is okay to be present. Be present as much as you can. Take your breaks and take your naps when needed.

When you become overwhelmed with feelings take a pause, pour it out, process, chilla, and shake it. We must *shake it shake it* to continue blossoming.

I am still on my medication. I am taking it one day at a time. If they are not needed, I don't take them. I am diminishing coffee and increasing water consumption.

I am jogging, stretching, and eating kale. I have even signed up for my second 5K. Sometimes things do not turn out how we want them to. Often, our justice system fails us. Orders for protection are nearly impossible to obtain, and unconnected white male judges blame us for loving and use this to discredit our strength. They perpetuate other abusers and neglect those that seek their expertise.

However, this is when the energy of the universe aligns to do its due diligence. The world works and it brings us wonders.

I am excited to continue learning and growing. I am peacefully closing this chapter of my life, one that sucked. However, it also taught me many lessons. Most importantly, it showed me what it means to be truly free and loved.

Libérate

Self-Care Monday
December 24, 2019

Self-care should not just be during the weekend. It should be during the weekdays too. It is the holiday season and I took yesterday off from work as a personal day.

A day for Michelle. Michelle Monday! Qué bonito.

I slept in and when my body was ready, I woke up and showered. I called to cancel my therapy appointment. Even though it is therapy, it is not the only self-care that is efficient in the healing process.

Therapy is not the only solution as a healthy state is also in need of medication, psychiatrists, counseling, or simply just a day for yourself. A healthy state of mind derives from acting and doing what feels right for you and your body.

After breakfast, a drink, and a pep-talk with Sandra, I was ready to make this happen and expand my horizons!

On Michelle Monday, I was going to do something I thought was wild, something I have wanted to do for the last two years but wasn't ready to do until now. I was going to do my hair at an actual salon with fancy shampoo names and products I've never even heard of. I was going to let someone care for me and make magic happen with my hair. What made it even more special was that it was Titi Karen doing my hair. The power of her energy and the goddess that she is, made this experience that much more significant.

I drove on the expressway and got lost twice. I had to give myself a pep-talk, but thankfully I got myself back on track.

Two and half hours later, I was a bolder me. I never understood the power of making drastic changes to yourself, mostly because I had never done something like this before. Now I know that it does make you feel more powerful, and more badass. Most importantly, it allows you to see yourself accomplishing other things. If I can do Rose Gold hair, I can do Rose Gold Publishing, and who knows what else I can do!

If I could take this small but significant step, it means I can do so much more!

Libérate

On my drive back, this came to mind: "Saborea cada pasito positivo que das."

And while driving, I found a pen and wrote it down on my hand. Not my safest approach but I just couldn't stop singing this in my head and I did not want to forget it. This is also another effect of enduring toxic behavior. Curioso, how our body is so interconnected.

"Saborea cada pasito positivo que das."

Sometimes the answers we are looking for are within our own body.

Sometimes, we need to step back and really listen to ourselves.

Sometimes, hasta nos sorprendemos nosotras mismas.

Libérate

Supporting Each Other
December 24, 2019

It is the holiday season and I have been reflecting on life. It has been two years in which every day that goes by, I realize que sí es mejor estar sola que mal acompañada. Sólo que, nunca estás sola.

Aunque a veces se sienta así, siempre tenemos a personas a nuestro alrededor que nos transmiten pensamientos positivos y energías curativas. Muchas veces, son extraños o personas que no lo expresan. Muchas veces, son nuestros padres.

I recently shared with my parents my publishing journey. To my surprise, they were supportive and very excited for me. Through talking with my momma, she shared that at one point in her life, she too wanted to be a published writer. However, life got in the way and she wasn't able to fulfill that dream.

What I realized is that we are not just our ancestor's wildest dreams, but we are our mom's wildest dreams. We can embark on journeys that were once and still might be too inconceivable to them. Sometimes, parents don't know how to process or understand our dreams and though they may come off as judgmental, they too are living this path with us. Our parents are healing through us. They are learning and exploring with us. It's up to us to honor the foundation they have provided us with by growing and thriving while remaining grounded.

Our life is not worth much if we are not reflecting and learning how to be of service to others and ourselves. This means that while we kick ass, it is important to slow down and realize that we are doing magical things. We can feel good about ourselves. We are magical beings. This is being peacefully beautiful. This is being in a mental place where we can look forward to life, set goals, and develop a path to thrive in life.

This is us.

Libérate

Final Thoughts:

Moments of Gratitude

Once upon a time, I was frustrated, negative, grouchy, and angry. After realizing how toxic I was being towards myself, I decided I had to focus that energy on more healthy approaches.

For a couple of months, I wrote down what I was grateful for each day. With a more conscious mind and heart, I was able to pull myself together and away from the sadness and stress I was going through. Here are a couple of things I am grateful for, listed in no particular order.

I Am Grateful To:

∞ Have a support system composed of family and friends.
∞ Be able to take risks and persevere.
∞ Face challenges and not give up.
∞ Sleep and make time to recharge.
∞ Choose kindness towards others and accept the kindness being given to me.
∞ Have time to rest and practice autonomy.
∞ Choose to be peaceful.

Libérate

- ∞ One way or another, seguir adelante and do so with a little bit of grace.
- ∞ Be breathing, alive and healthy.
- ∞ Never really be alone and to have a home.
- ∞ Be employed and earn income.
- ∞ Not have children to care for.
- ∞ Make time for reflection and growth.
- ∞ Have Sandra, her energy, and the role she has played in my life.
- ∞ Have courage to take risks and face challenges that often feel frightening.
- ∞ Be able to continuously build self-discipline and learn to embrace what I want my life to consist of.
- ∞ Have friends who support me and be able to surround myself with a new kind of love.
- ∞ My family and my kids (siblings).
- ∞ Have fresh starts.
- ∞ Be alive.
- ∞ Be able to experience moments of happiness.
- ∞ Understand my body enough to know I need to try anxiety and anti-depression medication.
- ∞ Be offered new opportunities.
- ∞ Be loved by others.
- ∞ Have room for growth, autonomy, self-love.

Libérate

∞ Receive affirmations and words of encouragement.
∞ Be part of genuine work and have humble intentions.
∞ Have women of color as my mentors.
∞ Have a community of love and accountability.
∞ Be able to volunteer and be part of a greater impact.
∞ Have aunts, uncles, and other extended family.
∞ Have a nonjudgmental brother-in-law who sets a good example for how other men should be.
∞ My brother's existence and soul that allows me to cultivate in him a pure, smart, compassionate, and badass male that will be able to carry out healthy relationships and end toxic cycles of fragile masculinity.
∞ Be able to be patient with myself.
∞ Have empowering conversations and to have spaces and people, to learn of different possibilities.
∞ Be able to seek professional help when needed and for the genuine people that remind you that it is not the end of the world and that things can and will get better because you have the power to make it happen.

Libérate

∞ Supervisors that are kind and give us a day off, allowing for a day to recuperate and practice self-care during a weekday.

∞ Have smooth closures leading to peaceful transitions

∞ Have friends that validate your experience and support you in your process.

∞ Sleep.

∞ Be able to realize my body needs more attention.

∞ Explore ways to rise from bad moods.

∞ Be a part of my community and to be surrounded by people that want a healthier version of themselves and a healthier community.

∞ Have social outings with friends and be welcomed into their homes.

∞ Have friends that help care for me and make sure I have slept and eaten.

∞ Those that remind you that you can only control so much and that you need to relax and breathe and trust the universe will help you solve your challenges.

∞ Make more time to celebrate life

∞ Share my truths and live in my reality.

∞ Be productive.

∞ Have extra hours of work.

∞ Have spent a few hours alone at home and not have an anxiety attack.

- ∞ Have slow starts.
- ∞ Have breakfast, take vitamins and see a brighter day.
- ∞ Family days and days spent at home.
- ∞ Have mental check-ins.
- ∞ Baby steps in reaching my future and professional goals.
- ∞ New beginnings and signs from the universe that assure us we are on the right path to a blissful life.
- ∞ Have moments of pureness such as being hugged in excitement by an intern at work just because she is also from El Salvador.
- ∞ Embrace life adventures: Having a bee enter your car while at the drive thru.
- ∞ Disfrutar que sí tengo pegue y soy coqueta.
- ∞ Have a healthier mental state than I did a year ago.
- ∞ Creating spiritual and energetic connections.

Your turn

I shared with you the past two years of myself. I hope it was helpful as my choice to do so came from a genuine place. However, it is also important for us all to continue thinking and having these conversations with ourselves and those around us. Treat these below as a living document; They are situational and ever changing.

Part of knowing how to care for yourself is being conscious of your stressors. What are somethings that trigger you? For me, loud noises are one of them. Knowing that, I let loud cars pass me or play my comfort music. Let's plan accordingly to make sure we always feel safe and secure.

What are some of your triggers?

1) _____

2) _____

How can we plan accordingly to make sure you feel safe and secure?

1) _____

2) _____

Develop your support plan

Libérate

Who is one adult you can confide in? Is it a family member or a friend? Why are they your go to person?

_____
_____
_____

Next steps in life

A former supervisor of mine had us do this activity. We take a moment to really think of ourselves and things we want to accomplish. We write them down on a note card or a sticky note. The key is to place this paper in your wallet, or a place where it won't disappear but is always reachable so as to serve as a daily reminder of what we are working towards. With that,

What are two personal goals you have?

(Examples: Jog X miles, drink more water, vacation)

1. _____
   _____
2. _____
   _____

Libérate

What are two professional goals you have? (Example: Enroll in higher ed., read more, explore a topic of interest? Secure better employment?)

1. _____
   _____

2. _____
   _____

Questions to reflect on

Are you at peace with yourself? What is one way to work towards that peaceful state we are all deserving of?

_____

_____

Are you living or surviving? Why?

_____

_____

Are you happy? Does your soul feel complete?

_____

_____

Palabras de mi Mamá:

"Si alguien dijera que la vida es fácil, sería porque no es de este mundo. A nivel de todos los tiempos la vida ha sido el mismo centro de la existencia en el cual el ser humano, ha caminado a su alrededor.

Sin embargo, los creyentes en un ser supremo han soportado y manipulado las palabras que nos han servido de guía y sabiduría. Pero al pasar el tiempo, la mente humana, las necesidades y las circunstancias han favorecido la vida y nuestro existir y nos han enseñado a que el ser humano es capaz de construir o destruir el precioso regalo de la vida.

Por esa razón al tener la libre decisión de pensar, razonar y amar a los demás nos lleva a ser mejores personas, evitando la violencia conyugal, familiar y mundial, si estamos en esta vida deberíamos buscar la forma de hacer de la existencia lo sublime, lo real, lo poderoso, lo irreal, para que todo lo existente, lo habitable, lo dado por un ser imaginario que llevamos todos dentro, a nivel celular y espiritual tenga el propósito original.

Libérate

El secreto de la vida a mi pensar se basa en el amor, en el amor a ti mismo como ser especial, a los demás, a cada partícula, molécula, átomo y en fin, todo cuanto existe y el agradecimiento al universo, a la luz proveedora de todo cuanto existe y el cual nos da lo necesario para subsistir. Si somos capaces de amar, seremos capaces de cambiar el mundo y nuestro planeta, empezando desde lo más profundo de nuestro ser.

Por esta razón y por mucho más, si sabemos apreciar nuestro alrededor, si podemos sentir la naturaleza y respetarla como algo único, si sabemos amar una flor, una hormiga, un ave, una nube, una lluvia, un arcoíris, aprendemos a vivir, a respetar a los demás , a nuestros prójimos, hijos, parejas, a cuanto existe y el amor y la verdad nos liberara y el mundo no sería mundo, sería la invención más increíble y fascinante que jamás nuestro imaginar habría registrado en lo más profundo de nuestro ser.

Siendo esa mi razón personal de concebir nuestra existencia."

-Angelica M. Calero

Libérate

Words from My Mother

If someone said that life was easy, it would be because they are not from this world. At the level of all time, life has been the same center of existence in which humans have walked around.

However, believers in a supreme being have endured and manipulated words that have served us as guidance and wisdom. But over time the human mind, needs and circumstances have favored life and our existence and have taught us that humans are capable of building or destroying the precious gift of life.

For that reason, having the free decision to think, reason and love others leads us to be better people, avoiding conjugal, family and global violence. If we are in this life we should look for ways to make existence sublime, the real, the powerful, the unreal, so that everything that exists, the habitable, that given by an imaginary being we all have inside, at the cellular and spiritual level have the original purpose.

The secret of life in my thinking is based on love, on the love of yourself as a special being, for others, for each particle, molecule, atom and in short, everything that exists and thanks to the universe, to the light providing everything that exists and which gives us what is necessary to survive. If we are able to love, we will be able to change the world and our planet, starting from the most profound part of our being.

For this reason and so much more, if we know how to appreciate our surroundings, if we can feel nature and respect it as something unique, if we know how to love a flower, an ant, a bird, a cloud, rain, a rainbow, we learn to live, to respect others, our neighbors, children, our partner, whatever exists. Love and truth will free us, and the world will not be a world, it would be the most incredible and fascinating invention that our imagination has ever registered in the most profound part of our being.

That being my personal reason for conceiving our "existence."

-Angelica M. Calero

Libérate

Gracias

Glossary

I consider Spanglish as a beautiful skill. It is a skill that merges our backgrounds and generations. It consists of words that are self-created or just feel right. It is mixing terminology from our parents' countries and making it our own. It is mixing el "cipote" del Salvador con el "escuincle" de México and English words.

Many of our forms of expression do not have a direct translation. Following are translations founded on cultural accuracy not scholarly or politically correct.

Libérate

WORDS

Spanish:	English:
Abuelita	Grandma
Abuelo	Grandfather
Algún	Some
Amigas/amigos	Friends
Cachets	Cheeks
Cada día	Everyday
Cafesito	Coffee
Chilla	Cry
Chillona	Crier
Chingona	Badass
Chingonas	Badass women
Curioso	Curious (interesting)

Libérate

Dulzuras	Sweet
Frijoles	Beans
Gloriosas	Glorious
Increíbles	Incredible
Libérate	Liberate yourself
Libertad	Freedom
Locura	Craziness
Los vecinos	The neighbors
Luchona	Fighter
Machismo	Male chauvinist
Mami	Mommy
Manitas	Little hands
Momento	Moment
Mujeres	Women

Libérate

Mujeres poderosas	Powerful Women
Ojitos	Little eyes
Papás	Parents
Papi	Daddy
Pero	But
Pesadillas	Nightmares
Piecitos	Little feet
Prima	Cousin
Qué bonito	How lovely
Suspiro	Sigh
Tías	Aunts
Terreno	Land
Tías y tíos	Aunts and uncles
Y con éso	And with that

About the Author

Michelle Ramirez moved to Cicero, IL at 10 years old. Her father is of Mexican background and mother is from San Salvador.

She currently resides in Cicero, IL. where she plans to continue learning, growing, and dedicating as much time as possible to her community.

In June 2017, Michelle graduated from DePaul University with a Double Major in Sociology and Latin American and Latino Studies. Upon graduation, Michelle spent the past two years growing and reflecting. During this time, she became aware of the importance of mental health and being connected to the needs of our bodies, minds, and souls. Through tough times, journaling really became her coping mechanism and those entries are now these experiences she shares. Michelle is considering a master's program for the near future and strongly believes in community engagement, voting, and completing the census count to ensure our community receives the support needed because we are worth of it. It is with the utmost genuine intentions, that Michelle hopes to be of service to her

Libérate

community while continuing to explore the
opportunities that life offers us.

Michelle is also one of the founding members
of **Rizoma Collective**, a recent Independent Political
Organization in Cicero. It is made up of community
members with the mutual goal of community,
transparency, and social justice. Please follow here:

Rizomacollective.com

- 131 -

LSF BROOKFIELD LIBRARY

Made in the USA
Las Vegas, NV
04 November 2021

33676010R00083